FIRESIDE

The Passionate Collector

Ellen Land-Weber

With an Introduction by Walter Benjamin

A FIRESIDE BOOK · PUBLISHED BY SIMON AND SCHUSTER · NEW YORK

A Fireside Book
Published by Simon and Schuster
A Division of Gulf & Western Corporation
Simon & Schuster Building
Rockefeller Center
1230 Avenue of the Americas
New York, New York 10020

FIRESIDE and colophon are trademarks of
Simon & Schuster

Designed by Eve Kirch
Manufactured in the United States of America

1   2   3   4   5   6   7   8   9   10

Library of Congress Cataloging in Publication Data

Land-Weber, Ellen.
    The passionate collector.

    (A Fireside book)
    1.   Collectors and collecting—United States—
Pictorial works.   I.   Title.
AM305.L36   790.1'32'0973   79–27630

ISBN 0–671–25254–2

For Julie, my favorite collector.

I want to extend a heartfelt thank-you to all of the gracious collectors who invited me into their homes, showed me their incredible possessions, told me their stories and allowed me to photograph.

Foreword

by Ellen Land-Weber

I have always been curious about people who collect things. All around me are the beginnings of many collections, but as there was never any focus or passion to the acquisition of these objects, I knew it wasn't the real thing. Then again, I sometimes wondered at my inability to return from an outing to the beach without pockets bulging with "treasures."

One day I realized that to be a photographer is to be a collector. All the photographs I had taken were sorted into categories; the subject of each had been actively pursued, persuaded or coaxed in whatever necessary and appropriate way to be part of the ever-growing accumulation. Rules were set, and occasionally broken, and the process of refinement, gaining knowledge of materials, history and techniques, and rejection of poor specimens in favor of seemingly better ones is unending and ever more involving.

I decided to collect collectors—photographically, of course. Since I didn't know any serious collectors personally, I asked a friend and was given the name of a young man in the next town who was an avid beer-can collector. I had never heard of such a thing and must admit to having felt a degree of skepticism. I waited about a year and then called him. He said, "Come on over," and during the several hours we spent together I not only learned to respect his passion for beer cans, but gained the first of several insights as to why people collect things with great dedication, purposefulness and ardor. Before I left he gave me the names of six other collectors, including his mother. Eventually I photographed four of them, each of whom gave me further names. This process kept repeating itself, which is the way I found about half the people in this book. The others I discovered through newspaper stories I collected for about a year, a few from magazine articles and the rest from simply asking just about everyone I met if he or she knew of an interesting collector. Many did.

Most of the hundred and fifty-two collectors I met and photographed were more than ordinarily cordial. Frequently they presented me with tokens of their collections before I left. The angel collector greeted me at the door with a huge angel-food cake baked for the occasion of my visit. The anvil collector made an ornamental iron marshmallow toaster to demonstrate the use of one of his anvils, and the escutcheon collector gifted me with an escutcheon and matching door-knob mounted on a mahogany base with a ball-point pen attached, for my desk.

I began by photographing people locally, in the rural Northern California county where I live. I was astonished at the extent and number of collections that turned up in such unpromising territory. But this turned out to be fairly typical. Collectors can be found everywhere. Over a two-year period, for the sake of a balanced view, I traveled through about forty states to collect collectors. Many collections reflect regional character, ex-amples being whiskey stills in North Carolina, gambling items in Nevada and clocks in Connecticut.

I spent between two and three hours with each person, occasionally much longer. I avoided dealers and institutional collections, setting as criteria that the collector be serious about collecting and that the collection be a personal one. "Serious" means that the collector devotes a good deal of time and energy to the collection, which often means all the spare money and much of the living space as well. "Personal" is simply how the collection is used, for one's own satisfaction rather than to make money.

Almost no one refused permission to be photographed. Of the few who did say no, two were unwilling to allow anyone to see their collections out of fear that thieves would learn of their whereabouts. (I promised everyone I photographed that I would not reveal names or locations to prevent this possibility.) And one art collector did not want to appear in the same book with perhaps a marble collector. She felt art collecting was of a different order altogether. It's not.

Perhaps it will be no surprise that as I met more and more collectors, certain shared personality characteristics became evident.

A great many collectors have a strong sense of and deep interest in history, some almost living in the past through their collections. The collection often serves as a vehicle for historical research via the path of its particular subject. This is even true of the collector of natural specimens such as butterflies, plants or fossils, the research undertaken in these cases being about evolutionary or geological changes in the history of a species or of the planet. Most collectors enjoy living with their collections all around them, usually on display in their homes, often in the more personal inner rooms.

Many have been collecting one thing or another all their lives; the nature of the collection may change, but the activity is a continuous, lifelong habit. Commonly, collectors have grown up in the midst of collecting families. And the subject of their collections is invariably related to either occupation, family history or childhood experiences.

The advanced collectors whom I met nearly always followed a well-defined pattern of development. The first stage, frequently occurring in childhood, is characterized by an indiscriminate gathering of objects, not necessarily on one subject, sometimes with the intent to have more than anyone else or every different example in existence of a particular item. At a certain point, often when all available storage and display space is exhausted, the collector begins to specialize, either by making the subject more specific (only flutes made between 1790 and 1840) or by raising the standards of acceptable quality (only perfect arrowheads), or both. This may require that the collection shrink significantly in size, while the pride and sense of accomplishment of the collector grow in inverse proportion. The hoarder-accumulator evolves into the connoisseur-curator. Concurrent with this process is the ever-increasing knowledge of the subject of the collection, gleaned from libraries, old catalogs, appropriate field trips, other collectors and especially from intimate familiarity with the collection itself.

The most commonly heard answers to the question "Why has collecting reached such vast proportions recently?" are that the phenomenon is a result of increased leisure, growing affluence and inflation, which has made collecting a good investment. Maybe those are factors, but they are not sufficient explanations.

There are plenty of other things to do with extra time and cash besides haunt flea markets and follow up obscure classi-fied ads—pursuits such as travel, athletics, bridge or good deeds. Besides, many of the people on these pages either do not have a great deal of leisure time or are of rather modest means (sometimes both). Income may determine *what* one collects, but seems to have no bearing on whether or not one is a collector. Nor does the investment idea hold up too well. While many collections do have high monetary value, they are not exactly liquid assets. What a collection may be worth on paper and converting it into cash are two different matters. Most of the collectors I met seem to be far more concerned with the eventual safekeeping of their accumulations, such as a home in a museum, than with money in the bank.

More to the point are the sense of personal accomplishment and the accompanying pride collectors seem to share. Collecting means that they relate to the world in a special way. Watch collectors in action and you see a certain look in their eyes. The will to acquire a desired new addition brings out every resource of ingenuity, even cunning, to gain it. And then there is the interesting possibility raised by two collectors I met that collecting is a vestigial instinctive behavior remaining from the earliest days of the human race when gathering and storing food were necessary for survival. As with all such instincts no longer subject to natural selection, it is stronger in some than in others and emerges only when conditions are favorable.

Perhaps collecting behavior is sparked

by a single memorable experience in one's past. Many collectors will tell you that their collecting activities began when they saw a particular item one day that really struck them in a special way. They simply had to have it, though few could tell you just why.

A conversation with a friend reminded me of a forgotten experience of this nature just as I was nearing the end of my own collecting trip. When I first became involved in photography I was in the habit of roaming the Iowa countryside in search of photogenic subject matter; having grown up in an Eastern city, I found the rural towns of the Midwest exotic. One day I stopped in a tiny village to take pictures of a big old farmhouse because its front lawn was decorated with

an extraordinary number of lawn ornaments. The woman of the house, who was probably in her late sixties, came out to see what I was doing and after talking awhile invited me inside, where I found a scene that filled me with strangely mixed feelings of admiration and horror.

Every available space on every wall and piece of furniture was covered with a profusion of horses and dolls. She collected dolls; her husband, horses. Dolls and horses of every conceivable size, age and quality were stacked, arranged, hung and otherwise displayed, sometimes many layers deep, leaving only a narrow passageway by which to navigate through each room. Only a couple of chair seats and one bed were spared. The house had eight or ten large rooms, all congested in

the same manner except for the kitchen, which appeared to be close to the point of submersion in dolls and horses as well. I was incapable technically and maybe emotionally to adequately photograph that incredible scene then.

Oddly enough, two weeks after being reminded of this experience (wondering how I could have forgotten it so completely while devoting nearly full time and thought to collectors), I was once again driving through Iowa, and although I thought I couldn't remember just where that house was, nevertheless I drove straight to it, after thirteen years.

I was too late. The doll-collecting woman's daughter and her husband are living there now. The doll woman had died three years earlier, but the dolls and horses had remained intact until her horse-collecting husband's death just two months before my visit. By that time the daughter had disposed of about half of this lifelong accumulation in several yard sales, filling the yard each time, and had plans to soon sell the rest in a similar manner.

My poor timing was a disappointment, but the rapid dismantling of this vast collection was not surprising. A collection is very much an extension of the life of the collector; the longer the life, the more intimate the bond. Inevitably, the collection will die in some fashion at the same moment as the collector.

Unpacking My Library

A Talk about Book Collecting

by Walter Benjamin

I am unpacking my library. Yes, I am. The books are not yet on the shelves, not yet touched by the mild boredom of order. I cannot march up and down their ranks to pass them in review before a friendly audience. You need not fear any of that. Instead, I must ask you to join me in the disorder of crates that have been wrenched open, the air saturated with the dust of wood, the floor covered with torn paper, to join me among piles of volumes that are seeing daylight again after two years of darkness, so that you may be ready to share with me a bit of the mood—it is certainly not an elegiac mood but, rather, one of anticipation—which these books arouse in a genuine collector. For such a man is speaking to you, and on closer scrutiny he proves to be speaking only about himself. Would it not be presumptuous of me if, in order to appear convincingly objective and down-to-earth, I enumerated for you the main sections or prize pieces of a library, if I presented you with their history or even their usefulness to a writer? I, for one, have in mind something less obscure, something more palpable than that; what I am really concerned with is giving you some insight into the relationship of a book collector to his possessions, into collecting rather than a collection. If I do this by elaborating on the various ways of acquiring books, this is something entirely arbitrary. This or any other procedure is merely a dam against the spring tide of memories which surges toward any collector as he contemplates his possessions. Every passion borders on the chaotic, but the collector's passion borders on the chaos of memories. More than that: the chance, the fate that suffuse the past before my eyes are conspicuously present in the accustomed confusion of these books. For what else is this collection but a disorder to which habit has accommodated itself to such an extent that it can appear as order? You have all heard of people whom the loss of their books has turned into invalids, or of those who in order to acquire them became criminals. These are the very areas in which any order is a balancing act of extreme precariousness. "The only exact knowledge there is," said Anatole France, "is the knowledge of the date of publication and the format of books." And indeed, if there is a counterpart to the confusion of a library, it is the order of its catalogue.

Thus there is in the life of a collector a dialectical tension between the poles of disorder and order. Naturally, his existence is tied to many other things as well: to a very mysterious relationship to ownership, something about which we shall have more to say later; also, to a relationship to objects which does not emphasize their functional, utilitarian value—that is, their usefulness—but studies and loves them as the scene, the stage, of their fate. The most profound enchantment for the collector is the locking of individual items within a magic circle in which they are fixed as the final thrill, the thrill of acquisition, passes over them. Everything remembered and thought, everything conscious, becomes the pedestal, the frame, the base, the lock of his property. The period, the region, the craftsmanship, the former ownership—for a true collector the whole background of an item adds up to a magical encyclopedia whose quintessence is the fate of his object. In this circumscribed area, then, it may be surmised how the great physiognomists—and collectors are the physiognomists of the world of objects—turn into interpreters of fate. One has only to watch a collector handle the objects in his glass case. As he holds them in his hands, he seems to be seeing through them into their distant past as though inspired. So much for the magical side of the collector—his old-age image, I might call it.

Habent sua fata libelli: these words may have been intended as a general statement about books. So books like *The Divine Comedy,* Spinoza's *Ethics* and *The Origin of Species* have their fates. A collector, however, interprets this Latin saying differently. For him, not only books but also copies of books have their fates. And in this sense, the most important fate of a copy is its encounter with him, with his own collection. I am not exaggerating when I say that to a true collector the acquisition of an old book is its rebirth. This is the childlike element which in a collector mingles with the element of old age. For children can accomplish the renewal of existence in a hundred unfailing ways. Among children, collecting is only one process of renewal; other processes are the painting of objects, the cutting out of figures, the application of decals—the whole range of childlike modes of acquisition, from touching things to giving them names. To renew the old world—that is the collector's deepest desire when he is driven to acquire new things, and that is why a collector of older books is closer to the wellsprings of collecting than the acquirer of luxury editions. How do books cross the threshold of a collection and become the property of a collector? The history of their acquisition is the subject of the following remarks.

Of all the ways of acquiring books, writing them oneself is regarded as the most praiseworthy method. At this point many of you will remember with pleasure the large library which Jean Paul's poor little schoolmaster Wutz gradually acquired by writing, himself, all the works whose titles interested him in book-fair catalogues; after all, he could not afford to buy them. Writers are really people who write books not because they are poor, but because they are dissatisfied with the books which they could buy but do not like. You, ladies and gentlemen, may regard this as a whimsical definition of a writer. But everything said from the angle of a real collector is whimsical. Of

13

the customary modes of acquisition, the one most appropriate to a collector would be the borrowing of a book with its attendant non-returning. The book borrower of real stature whom we envisage here proves himself to be an inveterate collector of books not so much by the fervor with which he guards his borrowed treasures and by the deaf ear which he turns to all reminders from the everyday world of legality as by his failure to read these books. If my experience may serve as evidence, a man is more likely to return a borrowed book upon occasion than to read it. And the nonreading of books, you will object, should be characteristic of collectors? This is news to me, you may say. It is not news at all. Experts will bear me out when I say that it is the oldest thing in the world. Suffice it to quote the answer which Anatole France gave to a philistine who admired his library and then finished with the standard question, "And you have read all these books, Monsieur France?" "Not one-tenth of them. I don't suppose you use your Sèvres china every day?"

Incidentally, I have put the right to such an attitude to the test. For years, for at least the first third of its existence, my library consisted of no more than two or three shelves which increased only by inches each year. This was its militant age, when no book was allowed to enter it without the certification that I had not read it. Thus I might never have acquired a library extensive enough to be worthy of the name if there had not been an inflation. Suddenly the emphasis shifted; books acquired real value, or, at any rate, were difficult to obtain. At least this is how it seemed in Switzerland. At the eleventh hour I sent my first major book orders from there and in this way was able to secure such irreplaceable items as *Der blaue Reiter* and Bachofen's *Sage von Tanaquil*, which could still be obtained from the publishers at that time.

Well—so you may say—after exploring all these byways we should finally reach the wide highway of book acquisition, namely, the purchasing of books. This is indeed a wide highway, but not a comfortable one. The purchasing done by a book collector has very little in common with that done in a bookshop by a student getting a textbook, a man of the world buying a present for his lady or a businessman intending to while away his next train journey. I have made my most memorable purchases on trips, as a transient. Property and possession belong to the tactical sphere. Collectors are people with a tactical instinct; their experience teaches them that when they capture a strange city, the smallest antique shop can be a fortress, the most remote stationery store a key position. How many cities have revealed themselves to me in the marches I undertook in the pursuit of books!

By no means all of the most important purchases are made on the premises of a dealer. Catalogues play a far greater part. And even though the purchaser may be thoroughly acquainted with the book ordered from a catalogue, the individual copy always remains a surprise and the order always a bit of a gamble. There are grievous disappointments, but also happy finds. I remember, for instance, that I once ordered a book with color illustrations for my old collection of children's books only because it contained fairy tales by Albert Ludwig Grimm and was published at Grimma, Thuringia. Grimma was also the place of publication of a book of fables edited by the same Albert Ludwig Grimm. With its sixteen illustrations my copy of this book of fables was the only extant example of the early work of the great German book illustrator Lyser, who lived in Hamburg around the middle of the last century. Well, my reaction to the consonance of the names had been correct. In this case too I discovered the work of Lyser, namely *Linas Märchenbuch,* a work which has remained unknown to his bibliographers and which deserves a more detailed reference than this first one I am introducing here.

The acquisition of books is by no means a matter of money or expert knowledge alone. Not even both factors together suffice for the establishment of a real library, which is always somewhat impenetrable and at the same time uniquely itself. Anyone who buys from catalogues must have flair in addition to the qualities I have mentioned. Dates, place names, formats, previous owners, bindings and the like: all these details must tell him something—not as dry, isolated facts, but as a harmonious whole; from the quality and intensity of this harmony he must be able to recognize whether a book is for him or not. An auction requires yet another set of qualities in a collector. To the reader of a catalogue the book itself must speak, or possibly its previous ownership if the provenance of the copy has been established. A man who wishes to participate at an auction must pay equal attention to the book and to his competitors, in addition to keeping a cool enough head to avoid being carried away in the competition. It is a frequent occurrence that someone gets stuck with a high purchase price because he kept raising his bid—more to assert himself than to acquire the book. On the other hand, one of the finest memories of a collector is the moment when he rescued a book to which he might never have given a thought, much less a wishful look, because he found it lonely and abandoned in the marketplace and bought it to give its its freedom—the way the prince bought a beautiful slave girl in *The Arabian Nights.* To a book collector, you see, the true freedom of all books is somewhere on his shelves.

To this day, Balzac's *Peau de chagrin* stands out from long rows of French volumes in my library as a memento of my most exciting experience at an auction. This happened in 1915 at the Rümann auction put up by Emil Hirsch, one of the greatest of book experts and most distinguished of dealers. The edition in question appeared in 1838 in Paris, Place de la Bourse. As I pick up my copy, I see not only its number in the Rümann collection, but even the label of the shop in which the first owner bought the book over ninety years ago for one-eightieth of today's price. "Papeterie I. Flanneau," it says. A fine age in which it was still possible to buy such a de luxe edition at a stationery dealer's! The steel engravings of this book were designed by the foremost French graphic artist and executed by the foremost engravers. But I was going to tell you how I acquired this book. I had gone to Emil Hirsch's for an advance inspection and had handled forty or fifty volumes; that particular volume had inspired in me the ardent desire to hold on to it forever. The day of the auction came. As chance would have it, in the sequence of the auction this copy of *La Peau de chagrin* was preceded by a complete set of its illustrations printed separately on India paper. The bidders sat at a long table; diagonally across from me sat the man who was the focus of all eyes at the first bid, the famous Munich collector Baron von Simolin. He was greatly interested in this set, but he had rival bidders; in short, there was a spirited contest which resulted in the highest bid of the entire auction—far in excess of three thousand marks. No one seemed to have expected such a high figure, and all those present were quite excited. Emil Hirsch remained unconcerned, and whether he wanted to save time or was guided by some other consideration, he proceeded to the next item, with no one really paying attention. He called out the price, and with my heart pounding and with the full realization that I was unable to compete with any of those big collectors, I bid a somewhat higher amount. Without arousing the bidders' attention, the auctioneer went through the usual routine—"Do I hear more?" and three bangs of his gavel, with an eternity seeming to separate each from the next—and proceeded to add the auctioneer's charge. For a student like me the sum was still considerable. The following

morning at the pawnshop is no longer part of this story, and I prefer to speak about another incident which I should like to call the negative of an auction. It happened last year at a Berlin auction. The collection of books that was offered was a miscellany in quality and subject matter, and only a number of rare works on occultism and natural philosophy were worthy of note. I bid for a number of them, but each time I noticed a gentleman in the front row who seemed only to have waited for my bid to counter with his own, evidently prepared to top any offer. After this had been repeated several times, I gave up all hope of acquiring the book in which I was most interested that day. It was the rare *Fragmente aus dem Nachlass eines jungen Physikers* [Posthumous Fragments of a Young Physicist] which Johann Wilhelm Ritter published in two volumes at Heidelberg in 1810. This work has never been reprinted, but I have always considered its preface, in which the author-editor tells the story of his life in the guise of an obituary for his supposedly deceased unnamed friend—with whom he is really identical—as the most important sample of personal prose

of German Romanticism. Just as the item came up I had a brain wave. It was simple enough: since my bid was bound to give the item to the other man, I must not bid at all. I controlled myself and remained silent. What I had hoped for came about: no interest, no bid, and the book was put aside. I deemed it wise to let several days go by, and when I appeared on the premises after a week, I found the book in the secondhand department and benefited by the lack of interest when I acquired it.

Once you have approached the mountains of cases in order to mine the books from them and bring them to the light of day—or, rather, of night—what memories crowd in upon you! Nothing highlights the fascination of unpacking more clearly than the difficulty of stopping this activity. I had started at noon, and it was midnight before I had worked my way to the last cases. Now I put my hands on two volumes bound in faded boards which, strictly speaking, do not belong in a bookcase at all: two albums with stick-in pictures which my mother pasted in as a child and which I inherited. They are the seeds of a collection of children's books which is growing steadily even today, though no longer in my garden. There is no living library that does not harbor a number of booklike creations from fringe areas. They need not be stick-in albums or family albums, autograph books or portfolios containing pamphlets or religious tracts; some people become attached to leaflets and prospectuses, others to handwriting facsimiles or typewritten copies of unobtainable books; and certainly periodicals can form the prismatic fringes of a library. But to get back to those albums: Actually, inheritance is the soundest way of acquiring a collection. For a collector's attitude toward his possessions stems from an owner's feeling of responsibility toward his property. Thus it is, in the highest sense, the attitude of an heir, and the most distinguished trait of a collection will always be its transmissibility. You should know that in saying this I fully realize that my discussion of the mental climate of collecting may confirm you in your conviction that this passion is behind the times, in your distrust of the collector type. Nothing is further from my mind than to shake either your conviction or your distrust. But one thing should be noted: the phenomenon of collecting loses its meaning as it loses its personal owner. Even though public collections may be less objectionable socially and more useful academically than private collections, the objects get their due only in the latter. I do know that time is running out for the type that I am discussing here and have been representing before you a bit *ex officio*. But, as Hegel put it, only when it is dark does the owl of Minerva begin its flight. Only in extinction is the collector comprehended.

Now I am on the last half-emptied case, and it is way past midnight. Other thoughts fill me than the ones I am talking about—not thoughts but images, memories. Memories of the cities in which I found so many things: Riga, Naples, Munich, Danzig, Moscow, Florence, Basel, Paris; memories of Rosenthal's sumptuous rooms in Munich, of the Danzig Stockturm where the late Hans Rhaue was domiciled, of Süssengut's musty book cellar in North Berlin; memories of the rooms where these books had been housed, of my student's den in Munich, of my room in Bern, of the solitude of Iseltwald on the Lake of Brienz and finally of my boyhood room, the former location of only four or five of the several thousand volumes that are piled up around me. O bliss of the collector, bliss of the man of leisure! Of no one has less been expected, and no one has had a greater sense of well-being than the man who has been able to carry on his disreputable existence in the mask of Spitzweg's "Bookworm." For inside him there are spirits, or at least little genii, which have seen to it that for a collector—and I mean a real collector, a collector as he ought to be— ownership is the most intimate relationship that one can have to objects. Not that they come alive in him; it is he who lives in them. So I have erected one of his dwellings, with books as the building stones, before you, and now he is going to disappear inside, as is only fitting.

I've been a book collector all my life. For many, many years I had the books stacked floor to ceiling, five rows deep, in a fourth-floor walk-up garret —you couldn't get to most of them. So building this library is a dream come true. The space is designed like a labyrinth, with my table here in the center.

I've just begun the enormous task of unpacking and organizing over 30,000 books and periodicals. The subject of my library is art, but the theme is fantasy. My interest is in the reaches and richness of the human mind, and any book exemplifying a highly unusual imagination is fit for my shelf. After all, isn't this what art is all about?

I have books in eleven categories: Architecture; Painting and Sculpture (with a big section on surrealism); Illustrated Books (especially fantasy); Photography; Physical Sciences; "Mental" Sciences, which includes parapsychology and strange phenomena; books on Bookmaking; Antiques; Sexology; Literary Works, which includes fiction, plays and poems, and Miscellaneous, which includes sociology and religion.

There is an intimate connection between my own work as a photographer and these books. My pictures would not be what they are were it not for the library.

19

I collect advertising pencils and pens. They can be wood, ball-point, bullet—in fact any type of writing instrument that advertises something. It began when I happened to look over a bunch of pencils I was getting for a collector friend of mine. The idea just kind of got to me, and twenty years later I'm still fascinated by it.

I have over 9,000 pencils, but some are my trading stock, for exchanges with out-of-state collectors. I find my pencil hobby very relaxing. It takes my mind off everyday problems.

My interest in insects began when I worked for a Hawaiian museum at its field station in New Guinea collecting animals and insects for study as possible disease carriers and for basic identification of species and their distribution. Most of the insects in the photograph are from New Guinea, with some from Asia, Australia and Africa.

I feel that collecting is a privilege and should never be carried to excess. Collecting a couple of specimens of each species is preferable to collecting a great many of one species.

Here I am surrounded by a small portion of my collection of maps of Transylvania, a principality that was an independent country from 1538 to 1707 and an integral part of the kingdom of Hungary from 896 until 1921, when the Peace Treaty of Trianon gave it to Romania.

According to books and documents in my possession, my family lived in that part of the world since the late 8th or early 9th century. When my ancestors arrived as Chinese silk tradesmen from a place called Bihar, India, according to Chinese custom they named the place they settled the same way, Bihar. Three families wandering together settled there, intermarried with the Hungarians and have lived there ever since. On my father's side,

members of the family occupied the same building from the mid 1400s until it was totally destroyed near the end of World War II.

There were always a couple of maps of Transylvania at home, but I don't recall anyone in the family collecting them. I began the collection shortly after World War II and have continued up to the present in a systematic fashion, trying to purchase every available map from every known atlas and work on cartography up until 1850.

I always suspected this collection was pretty good, but now that the leading world authority on the subject of maps has examined it and told me it's the best in existence, I know so.

My husband and I went on expeditions to ghost towns with another couple for about fifteen years to hunt for old bottles. When we found a good spot, we'd divide up the area; then whatever was found in your territory belonged to you. The site of an old latrine was one of the best places to look, especially for whiskey bottles.

Although we have found every imaginable type of bottle, the canning jars have become my own specialty.

I had the idea to start this collection in 1942 when I first came to this valley. I have about 2,000 hubcaps. I really enjoy it when people come to look.

Clothing interests me a great deal, but especially men's hats. I collect every type of male headgear, except for military and law-enforcement, from all over the world.

Few people these days realize the way clothes used to be made. The enormous amount of time and craft required for the exquisite needlework and the fineness and luxury of the fabrics resulted in clothing that could never be duplicated today. These are just a few items in my extensive collection of fine antique clothes.

The collection began when I inherited the gowns my fashionable grandmother had made for her in Paris at the turn of the century.

Shown here are Hawaiian shirts from the 1930s to the 1950s, most made entirely of rayon. Since collecting the shirts can easily be overwhelming, I've limited myself to the more unique and rare shirts, which also must fit me. I'm very selective and won't buy a shirt unless it really strikes me. Some collectors won't wear their shirts, but I enjoy the fact that my collection is functional.

As a designer I have always looked at pattern as a source of inspiration. Hawaiian shirt patterns are much more than abstract designs. Most of the patterns are figurative and indigenous only to Hawaii, reflecting Hawaiian history, legend and lore.

Everything I collect might be called pinups of the 1920s through 1940s. There is a special image of women here which intrigues me.

I began collecting bits about ten years ago after seeing another man's collection. These were used for workhorses, and no two are alike.

Why sewing machines? They are mechanically ingenious and were produced in a seemingly endless variety of styles and designs. Since they are often found in dismal condition, the restoration of the machine heads and cabinets becomes a rewarding challenge.

There are 70 to 80 machines in the house now, mostly treadle, and all but 10 are in good working order.

I always used to think it would be nice to fix up a little house in an old railroad car. In 1962 I had the opportunity to buy the first two, the *Stag Hound* and the *Great Republic*, from the Yankee Clipper line that ran between Boston and New York, and I restored them instead. Originally there were fourteen cars on that train, each named after a famous clipper ship. These are all that remain.

The land here was wilderness then. I cleared it and laid the track. I had to hire house movers to bring the cars up.

The following year I bought two more, including the parlor car I'm sitting in. Then in 1964, car fever struck again and I bought a Pullman sleeper and an observation car, which is now situated so that its platform overlooks the tracks of the main Washington–Boston run, a few dozen yards away.

I'm in the midst of painting and restoring all of them to their original condition.

In the winter I work on the model trains which take up the whole top floor of my house. The tracks run from room to room through holes I cut in the walls for that purpose. I probably have a couple of thousand cars and engines up there.

Nuts have been speaking to me for a long time. Each one has a heart; every one is an idea.

I founded the nut museum seven years ago to elevate the nut from a mere edible delight to a higher plane of appreciation. My original idea was to house the collection in a building shaped like a walnut. Since that hasn't worked out, it is presently in my home. The only problem I have had is with the chipmunks and squirrels. They have carried off over fifty exhibits.

When I was a child I remember we always had bowls of nuts around the house. I realized at an early age that they were more than cold fossils. They are fresh examples of primeval existence, because they look ancient, but are renewed annually.

I am of Armenian heritage. Undoubtedly this accounts for my passion for nuts. Nuts supposedly originated in Old Armenia, which is also the conjectured site of the Garden of Eden. I'm convinced Eve didn't give Adam an apple, it was a nut.

The griffin is a mythic creature with the head of a lion and the body of an eagle. According to tradition, the griffin appeared mysteriously to serve as guardian to the gods who used their powers wisely and for good purposes. If one turned to evil deeds, the griffin disappeared.

Griffins have another mysterious quality—that of being unseen. People come to my house and may spend several hours and never become conscious of being surrounded by griffins, about two thousand of them.

It was the shapes of the duck decoys that first attracted me to them, not hunting and shooting. There are still some fine craftsmen carving them, but making decoys for practical use is a dying art.

Our collection began when Nina inherited a 52-horse carousel, intact but deteriorated, from her father, who had been a roller-coaster designer. As we set about restoring the horses we became interested in the history of the carvers and the carousels, and we began to augment our carousel by trading and doing restoration work for other collectors— there are about three hundred in the United States.

At first we wanted only animals carved by Gustav Dentzall, a German immigrant who founded the first American company in 1867. He carved our original carousel. As our knowledge of the carvers and the peculiarities of their various styles grew, our tastes expanded and we began to add other examples to the collection.

American carousel carving flourished in the brief period between 1880 and 1920, when the combination of new steam-powered and electric mechanisms and the development of "trolley parks" at the ends of the urban railway lines created keen competition for an ornate and brilliant "showpiece of the park" in towns and cities throughout the country. The animals represent a little-recognized but distinct achievement in American folk art. We take pride in helping to preserve it.

I always hunted small game and birds when I was a boy. I had my first chance at a big-game animal in 1938. It was a deer, and I got hooked on the adventure of taking it. Since then I've been all over the world. I have big-game animals from Africa, India, Siberia, the Yukon, British Honduras and North America and South America.

Hunting big game is all over now. The conservation movement has put an end to it.

My professional duty with the Department of Fish and Game is to protect the fish and wildlife resources in the state. Without a doubt, this spurred my interest in collecting steel traps.

I recognized that some traps were becoming rare because legislation has banned the use of those with barbs and teeth that meet in the middle—they do too much damage to an animal.

I have representative examples of every size from a 55-pound Newhouse No. 5 bear trap down to a little one for a mole, but I'm particularly interested in the larger bear traps and those which are homemade. These are the hardest to find and the most appealing to a collector because they were designed out of necessity with whatever talents and materials were at hand.

I collect anything relating to the history of the West, but especially Nevada. Everything in this room was collected by the time I was 18, and there's a lot more I've acquired since them.

When I was 8 I was given some family Civil War items. Then I found some guns and swords on my own and I became a real collector. I have Indian war items and mountain man things.

Everything in the photo is the paraphernalia of the gambler in the 19th and early 20th centuries, including faro boards, case counters, card presses, card trimmers, keno goose, a slot machine, guns and knives. Gaming has always fascinated me. Most of my collection comes from Nevada.

I never threw away my comic books when I was a kid. I find a lot about the values of our society in them, especially in Uncle Scrooge.

I began the collection because my parents are collectors and I wanted to have something of my own.

I collect advertising shoehorns, all different, some in combination with buttonhooks, bottle openers, combs and the like. They usually don't cost much, and they're fun to collect.

I've collected the algae, shells and shell fossils myself, mostly in California, some almost outside my door.

I think, upon reflection, that I have always collected "treasures." Myriad things have fallen into the treasure category over the years, including rocks, insects, shells, animal pictures, butterflies, feathers, books, live animals, seeds and bones. I discovered bones when I was an undergraduate in college and continue to find them quite diverting.

Animals have always piqued my curiosity, and so I surround myself with them or reminders of them lest I forget how incredible life is.

Dolls have fascinated me for as long as I can remember. Starting a doll collection may have been in my mind at the age of 6 or so, when I covertly made off with a friend's doll and was apprehended by the authorities, my parents, who convinced me that I had hardly employed the ideal method of commencing an enjoyable hobby. My present, and more honestly acquired, collection began in earnest in 1970 when my husband became curious about my absorption in dolls and encouraged me to become a collector.

Dolls are as varied as people. They come in all sizes, shapes, colors and personalities. Those shown here typify the dolls produced in Europe (mainly France and Germany) between 1870 and 1925. Most of this group have bisque heads, wigs of human hair or mohair, lifelike eyes of blown glass and bodies of jointed composition parts or leather stuffed with sawdust. One of the baby dolls is made of poured wax, and two or three all-wood dolls may also be seen in the photograph.

That these products of mundane materials somehow manage to develop human character is enchanting to me. It is a mystery further deepened by their antiquity. Long ago, I know, someone else was charmed by the old doll I see today; tomorrow her silent forces will capture another. Thus the antique doll holds claim to times past, present and future.

Our specialty is pictures of midgets. As our acquisitions increased in number we found ourselves ever more deeply immersed in researching the role of the "little people" in history. We've been able to identify a great many of the subjects of our pictures and have learned many of their stories. Strangely, the midgets themselves don't know their own history.

I had a lovely childhood, with many beautiful and wonderful toys, only a few of which have survived. I look for playthings that either are similar to those I had or remind me of them.

This is my small but personally important collection of cowboy memorabilia relating to the movies of my childhood. Roy, Gene and Hoppy symbolized a romantic ideal of manhood and were at the heart of many fantasies. Collecting these items helps keep memories of those fantasies alive.

Most of my badges are from Nevada law-enforcement and security agencies, and they reflect a good deal about the history of this area. The sheer number of different badges is astounding. I've put this collection together in about three years of very active hunting.

I often tell people that we collect antique fire-fighting equipment because my mother never bought me a fire truck, but that isn't strictly true.

We do have the best private collection in this part of the state. In the garage and next door are the big items—the pumper, which we fully restored, and the hand-drawn hose wagons. We've devoted about a year to the very careful restoration of one of the hose wagons, but it's not quite finished.

The real firehouse is two doors away. I'm the Fire Marshal.

My immigrant status, at the age of one, meant that I did not have an American heritage. This may be the reason I collect early American advertising.

Years ago, when I was involved in slum clearance, I became curious about why and how the slums had developed in the first place. In the course of searching for informative material, I would look for old ads at some of the long-established New England printing firms. I discovered how interesting graphically the early advertising was, and how much it revealed about the rise and spread of industrialization. I began picking up good examples here and there and soon had a collection. It was better than a college course in American history.

I was raised by an elderly woman in a home loaded with Victorian bric-a-brac, and grew up loving those crazy things. Then for six years I was the live-in caretaker/curator of an elegant Victorian house containing the most complete intact collection of original period furnishings in America. When it fell into the hands of an heiress who broke it up and sold everything at auction and yard sales, I could have cried.

Someday I hope to open my own Victorian home museum. I already have enough to fill it.

Being a professional photographer, I was naturally interested in photographic history. Collecting original items is a good way to learn. I've concentrated mostly in daguerreotypes, the earliest widely used photographic process and in some respects still the most perfect.

I've never been interested in being a photographer and so have never used any of my cameras. I've just always liked old cameras, especially the larger wooden ones.

Do you want to know what collecting is about in two words? Ego trip. That's it.

I'm in the store-fixture business. My dad had the same business before me. We used to have a lot of these old cash registers around—sometimes painted them brown to make them look more like wood. We felt pretty smug if we could foist one off on someone for $30 or $40.

Here's how I started my collection: I had an especially beautiful old cash register which I begged a young couple to buy for a boutique they were opening up. I wanted $100 for it, but they thought that was too much. So I told them, "You give me a hundred dollars and put the cash register in your store and if you don't make money I'll buy it back from you for a hundred dollars anytime." So they took it and then made a fortune. A year later I tried to buy it back for a $1,000, but they wouldn't sell. I'd still like to have that register back.

I always liked the old stuff, never did like anything new.

Steam-driven tractors went out around 1925 to 1935, when the gas-powered tractors took over, but I used one way up until 1956. Of course, if they had rubber tires on them, they'd be cheaper to run today than gas-powered machines.

In Pennsylvania, there might have been one of these every five or six miles. Out West, where the farms run hundreds of acres, you'd find lots of them. When a farmer quit using one, he would likely as not just run it over a cliff and let it rust. That's where you'll find them today.

In the picture from front to back you see a 16-horsepower Peerless TT, 1913; a 24-horse, 1923; a 12-horse Peerless R, 1894; a 25-horse Peerless Z, 1910; a 15-horse Peerless S, 1913, and a 12-horse Case, 1914.

I always have collected one thing or another. Jazz records, Norman Rockwell illustrations and circus items have all been serious interests—and as a matter of fact, still are.

However, my active collecting is currently in the area of wind-up toys, and within that I find myself beginning to specialize in just military and autos. I suppose as the collection keeps growing I'll have to make a decision between those two.

I'm happiest if the toys are out where my friends and I can see them.

I was always interested in the old-time crawler tractors, and one day I started buying them and fixing them up. I have at present about 30 old Caterpillar, Holt-Best, Allis-Chalmers and Monarch crawler tractors, all fixed up, painted and in operating condition. These are all different models—no duplicates. I also have 190 cast-iron implement seats, also all in perfect condition—no duplicates, all different.

We built the garage first and then attached the house to it. We have in here Cadillacs from 1937 to 1976, representing twenty-one different years, as well as dealership signs, fixtures, magazine ads, advertising pens, paper plates—anything pertaining to Cadillacs. We are not restorers; we save cars we find in excellent condition and do not "bring them back to life." We are not dealers; we never sell, trade or upgrade the collection by getting rid of one for another model.

Why we do it is always the hardest thing to answer.

There are two thousand Edsel lovers in this country, a couple in South America, one in Nicaragua and one in New Zealand. No one has ever denied that I'm the number one collector.

Edsels were made in 1958, 1959 and for three months in 1960. Only seventy-six convertibles were made in 1960. I have the one remaining of the two sold in this county.

The particular joy I get out of it is finding a car I'm told won't run, that has been sitting around for maybe ten years, and then taking it home and putting it back in running order.

Of course, I won't drive it again after that. If I drove my cars every day they'd get worn out. Ford doesn't make the parts anymore.

As of the day of this picture I have 2,715 different bells (but probably 5,000 altogether), including cowbells, school bells, a trolley-car bell and decorative bells of every size and description.

My interest in bells began in 1940 when my sister gave me one for my birthday. Since my middle name is Belle, making a collection seemed to be a good idea.

The collection consists of items one might have found in a country store around 1900. Everything I've collected is brand-new merchandise in the original boxes and packages. I remodeled this building as an old store to display everything, trying to be authentic in every detail including exposed wiring and period fixtures. There's so much, I've divided it into departments such as dry goods, groceries, shoes, patent medicines and livery, as well as a complete barbershop in the back.

As a longtime museum worker I became familiar with many Native American handcrafted objects. As an artist I have always been deeply appreciative of the designs and craftsmanship in these objects. My chief pleasure in this collection is that it serves as an inspiration for my own creative work.

I've lived on this Indian reservation for thirty years. Some of my beadwork bags were memorial gifts bequeathed by Indian friends. Others I bought directly from the Indians or at pawnshops.

With the way that values have shot up lately, it makes me nervous to have so much around. In a few years I'll probably give my whole collection to a small museum that needs some help.

A friend of ours began to collect Mickey Mouse in the 1950s and now has a *very* valuable collection. By the time we became interested in collecting, Mickey was far out of our price range, so we had the idea of collecting Snoopy. No one values Snoopy as a collectible now, which makes acquiring him very inexpensive and a lot of fun. We buy at flea markets, yard sales—even the neighborhood kids bring us Snoopy presents. At Christmas we give each other new Snoopy gifts. We call this our retirement fund.

Snoopy is 25 years old and does show signs of age. He used to be more of a dog; now his paws have turned into hands, and his expression, which used to look simpleminded, now looks sharp and intelligent.

A friend and I had a bet going as to who could obtain more credit cards in his name in one year. I managed to get 96 and won. I wondered if I had set a record, so I called up the *Guinness Book of World Records* and was told that since there was no such category, I probably had. This inspired me to keep going, and I now have over 900 different cards, all in my name, including one that will let me charge a house mortgage and one made of sterling silver for a Nevada casino.

The insurance people have told me that the $50 liability limitation in case of theft doesn't apply in my case, so I am forced to keep the collection in a safe-deposit box.

My next idea is to have the world's longest wallet.

The cans behind my right shoulder represent my specialty, which is any item from a California brewery. The oldest is from 1935, and almost all are obsolete, many companies having died with the Grace Brothers Brewery and the Maier Brewery in the middle '60s.

One of my chief joys in collecting breweriana is meeting other collectors. I began collecting cans in a casual manner when I worked in a liquor store. A few years later I read an article about other collectors and their club. I immediately joined and thereafter began to seriously build my collection.

My membership number is 1016, out of over 16,000 current members.

In 1962 our highway department experimented with a license plate with reflective indented letters and numbers on a reflective background. At night, the plates became big red reflectors—no one could read them. I was issued one of these and knew that it would become a rare item. This was the start of my collection. I have a South Carolina plate from every year except 1918, and I know I'll get that one sooner or later.

From 1917 to 1932, license plates in my state cost $18 to $20 a year. It was quite an expense. Olin D. Johnson ran successfully for governor in 1932 on a license-plate platform. He lowered the price to $3.60 and also allowed six-month plates, which helped out the farmers who couldn't afford a whole year's fee at one time.

I did the clubhouse in plates in 1975. The stars are painted on the backs of blue plates. I have enough green ones to redo the whole background when the blue ones get too faded.

The biggest whiskey still I've got holds 800 gallons. I call it "Big Boy." I paid a man $200 for it when it was three-quarters buried in the riverbed. After we dug it out, I paid a Traphill boy another $200 to clean and recondition it. When the work was almost done, I got scared the revenuers might get the wrong idea. I'm too old to go to jail. I invited them out to see it, and they said I could keep it if I chopped holes in the bottom to make it inoperable, which is what I did.

This county was famous for its illegal whiskey. There are probably some families back in the hills still making corn liquor, but it's a thing of the past. With all the new plants in the area, those boys can hold regular jobs now and make a lot more than they ever did with the whiskey.

O ne day when I was 16 I found my uncle beating some rugs with a very old tennis racquet. He didn't realize what it was. So I made him a rug beater and asked if I could have the old racquet in exchange. He agreed. That racquet was made in the 1780s and is still one of the best in my collection.

I was impatiently waiting for a friend to finish browsing through an antique store when I opened a drawer and discovered seven or eight unusual whistles. They kind of struck me. I bought them all—and then began years of searching for whistles of unusual design and origin, wherever we traveled.

Those in the glass case are made of chased sterling silver and coral and are combination whistles and baby rattles, made for well-off infants in the last century.

I was always interested in history, and I think that gave me the idea, about forty-five years ago, to start collecting antique tools. I began with old wrenches, but now I have lots of other collections as well.

I spend most of my time out here sorting, arranging and puttings things in order. It gives me great pleasure.

About forty years ago I got interested in collecting a few items that were common when I was a boy so that the younger generation could see some tools and devices that are no longer used.

At the extreme top left are four pairs of ice skates, one made in 1880. Next in line are four bullet molds and a shot pouch, brand new, marked 50 cents. The wheel-like thing is a device to measure the circumference of a wagon wheel. At bottom center is a harpoon hayfork, and between the tines of the hayfork is a rough lock for a freight wagon; at bottom right is a wagon jack.

I collect matchbooks only from places I've been myself. I won't accept gifts.

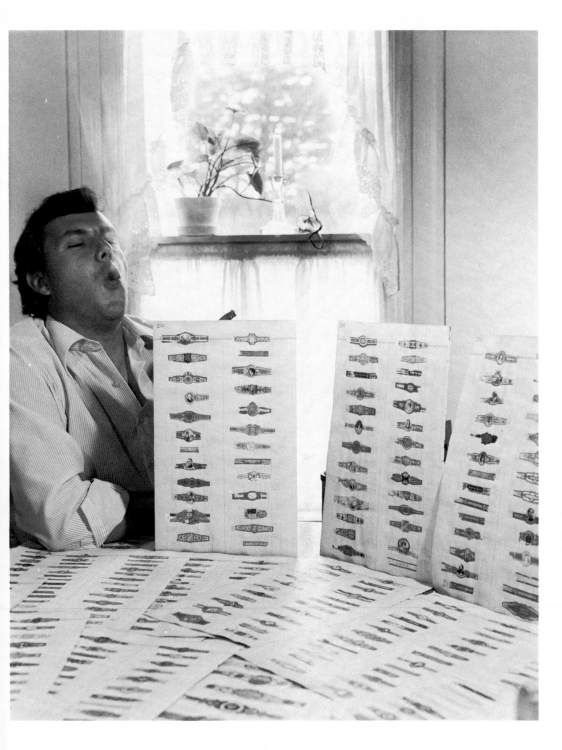

I inherited this collection of cigar bands from my maiden great-aunt who never smoked or drank, and I've been adding quite a bit to it whenever I can.

About twenty years ago I saw a package of Venus-flytrap "bulbs" in a store and bought them for $1. I still have the same plants today, although they have divided many times. Several years later I saw the carnivorous-plant collection at the University of California Botanical Gardens and begged a very small offshoot of a *Sarracenia* hybrid, which I also still have today. My collection remained stable at two species until the *Carnivorous Plant Newsletter* group became established about six years ago. This opened up a means of communication with other growers. I then developed an international seed and plant exchange in which several hundred growers exchanged information and plants. My collection quickly expanded to a couple of hundred species, which includes some of the rarest carnivorous plants in the world.

Collecting rare and endangered plants can be beneficial if it is conducted with care and knowledge. Carnivorous plants are generally found in wet, boggy places, viewed as undesirable for urban or agricultural use and therefore being drained and filled increasingly often. There are now several species of carnivorous plants which no longer exist in the wild, but only in a few cultivated collections.

Three principal genera are shown in the photo. In the foreground is a portion of a *Heliamphora*, a plant native only to the high mountain plateaus of Venezuela. The majority of the plants shown are of the genus *Sarracenia*. These pitcher plants are generally found only in the southeastern United States; however, one species, *Sarracenia purpuria*, ranges into northeastern Canada. The hanging plants are of the genus *Nepenthes*, found throughout southeast Asia and the western Pacific. The large carnivore in the background is not one of the plants, but the collector.

On the screen and in the framed picture are photomicrographs of one-celled microscopic water plants belonging to the class of algae called diatoms. Diatoms flourish in all the waters of the earth, wherever conditions are suitable. Over 15,000 species have been studied and classified, most before 1900.

The arrangement of microscopic diatoms in a symmetrical pattern is a source of sheer pleasure for many microscopists. It is done, of course, under the microscope by the simple but highly delicate technique of moving each diatom into place by hand with a cat's whisker or other suitable hair or filament of glass.

The peak of perfection in this art was reached by J. D. Rinnboeck of Vienna, who did his work about seventy-five years ago. Many of his masterpieces are in the hands of collectors today, and they are of wondrous beauty.

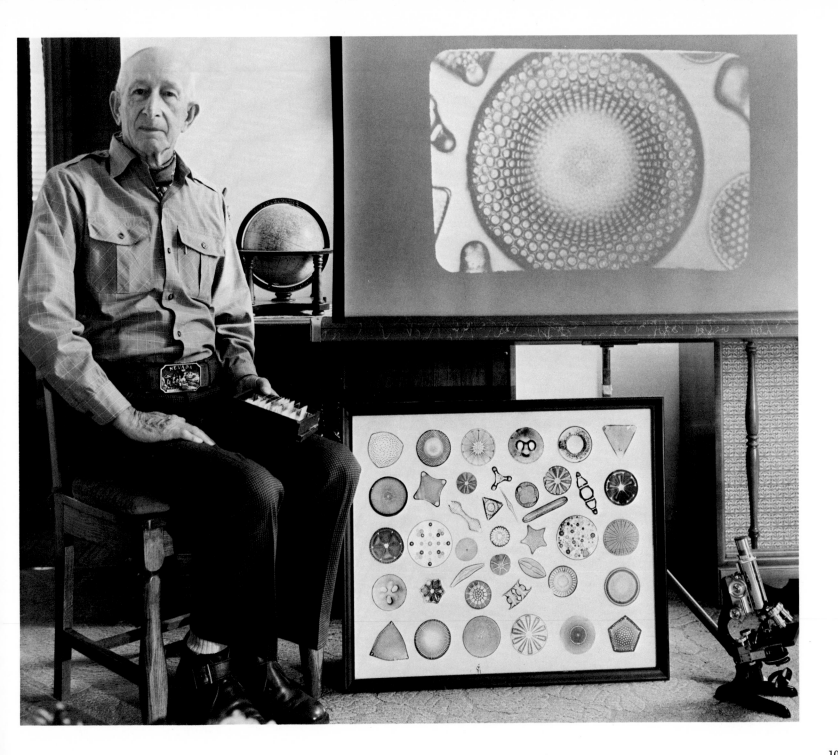

I suppose the mothering instinct is involved in our collection of Raggedy Anns. We've not only named each one but also given them occupations, such as truck driver, ditchdigger and waiter.

It started about three years ago at a country-church rummage sale. We bought a Raggedy Ann for 25 cents, and another "child," since named "Little Popeet," for 5 cents. The collection just grew and grew, largely from the compassion we feel whenever we find one lying neglected in a flea market or junk store. It's like greeting a long-lost friend. They and we equally share the joy.

My interest is in doorknobs, escutcheons, hinges and window lifts. I also have over 170 old catalogues which are invaluable for identifying each item by style, year and manufacturer.

My field is forensic locksmithing for the police department, which means identifying tools from the examination of evidence recovered at the scene of a crime. Naturally, I was always thinking about locks and keys, so when I first saw a beautifully ornate old escutcheon plate I wanted to have it.

There used to be loads of such plates at the flea markets, but since people started fixing up and restoring the older homes they're becoming more scarce.

I can truthfully say I am a true collector. I will first attempt to trade for an item I don't have; if that fails, I try to buy it; if these methods fail, I will atempt to obtain the item by any means whatever. As far as I know I am the only collector of this particular ornamental hardware in the world.

I had a feeling when *Catch-22* first came out that it was a special book. Not just the content, but that intense blue of the paperback cover really made it stand out on the store shelf. I began to pick up secondhand copies and noticed that with every new printing there would be subtle changes in the cover design. Sometimes the shade of blue varied a bit; other times a new line such as "over one million sold," then "over two million sold," would be added. I collected 26 different printings produced between 1962 and 1968.

When the movie was made, the meaning of the story seemed to change, as did the paperback jacket design, so I stopped collecting copies of *Catch-22* and concentrated on my key-chain collection instead.

I wanted to collect something that reflected our culture, that no one else was collecting and that didn't cost much. Lunch boxes are a capsule history of children's movie and television idols. I keep half my collection here and half at another location, just in case.

The jars were used for pickles, sugar and jams. The double ones would be filled with hard and soft sugar, sweet and sour pickles or two varieties of jam. They are pretty scarce, because the glass manufacturers stopped making the originals around 1900. I began buying them in 1929, which is why my collection consists almost entirely of originals. So many good copies are on the market, it often takes an expert to detect the difference.

I began at first collecting just the pickle jars, but this is a strange hobby, and other glass items appeared I felt I could not live without. My collection soon grew to mammoth proportions. A true collector is also a hoarder. Each item seems to be such an important part of one's life; one hangs on to it until there's scarcely room for everything. I am at that stage right now, wondering who will appreciate and give loving care to these priceless things as I have done.

In the 1930s and '40s a number of commercial potteries produced simple, brilliantly colored sets of dinnerware designed to express the then popular "machine esthetic." The idea was to celebrate the miracle of modern technology by employing clean lines and strictly functional shapes.

In spite of aspirations to pure functionalism, fantastic shapes often showed up in the pitchers and teapots. These are my favorites.

Everything we collect is "R.F.D."—Rescued From the Dump. Pictured here are a few examples of the over 500 different carriage and buggy steps we've found. We've published what is probably the most complete description of these steps, but we are always on the lookout for new ones.

We take pride in having achieved something no one else has done and having done it well. I think the collecting spirit in human beings was slowly built up by natural selection. For hundreds of thousands of years survival depended upon gathering, accumulating and eventually storing food for the winter or lean times. A hundred or so generations won't wipe out an ancient instinct.

I think the flamingo represents an exotic and flamboyant escape from the ho-hum everyday world, much as the peacock did in an earlier period.

It's very important to me to live with my flamingo collection all around me. All of these things are truly alive because they once belonged to someone else and now belong to me. I try to find out who owned each item I acquire, where it has been, how it was used, where it was kept in the house. If I trade or sell something, I try to keep track of it so that I can be sure the new owners will care for it as I have.

Our collection is concentrated on pianos, flutes, clarinets and horns made between 1790 and 1840, which was a period of great technological development for these instruments. We have between 350 and 400. We have not gone in for strings, Renaissance or ethnic instruments. Life is too short.

I am an organologist, which is a person who engages in the study of musical instruments. I may not play as a virtuoso, but I can possess the entire orchestra in my home.

Most of my instruments are ethnic. I also collect native folk music by tape-recording on field trips to places in Appalachia.

Collecting may be an instinctive behavior. I read an article in *National Geographic* about the bower-bird, which picks up any little thing it can find that's blue. Each bird makes a display of its blue objects, and if one likes something in another's collection, it will swoop in and grab it.

My father was apprenticed to a blacksmith in Vienna, and when he came to this country he established his own blacksmith business. I was apprenticed to my father's first helper. Two of my three brothers are still in the business.

I began to collect anvils about fifteen years ago, wanting every one I could find, from little two-inch ones, which were used as calling cards by people in ironwork, all the way up to one that weighs 515 pounds. I developed a kind of radar that allowed me to ferret out anvils wherever I went. I started the collection because it was a challenge—they're hard to find, and when you do find one it's not always for sale, no matter what you offer.

I like the shape of them. You can tell what period they come from by the different shapes. My oldest is from the 16th century.

I've run into ten or eleven other serious anvil collectors.

This is the world's biggest ball of string.

When I was a custom hay baler, I used to save the leftover bits and pieces of baling twine when it snarled up, which happened a lot. I saw a man on the TV who was making a ball of twine, and that gave me the idea. That was in 1950.

For twenty years I rolled up my ball with bumper jacks. Then my nephew built me a hydraulic roller. You can't just wind the twine around one way or you'll get a kind of hump in it. There's solid twine all the way through, though there might be a few acorns inside, since the squirrels like to sit on it. It's been in the *Guiness Book of World Records* five times.

I heard about a man in Kansas who also has a ball of twine, so I took a trip to see it. Mine is bigger.